When Flamenco is not Enough!
Healing Los Gitanos

Nerea San José Marqués

ISBN:1544140525
ISBN-13: 978-1544140520

DEDICATION

My gratitude to Filadelfia church for allowing me to be part of their lives for a few days.

Content

ACKNOWLEDGMENTS

This research was submitted as an essay for a course: Post Graduate Certificate in Cultural Diversity in Therapy; run by Goldsmith College, University of London (July 2005).

Preface

The aim of this book is to bring the Romany community and the therapist closer together. It gives general information about Romany rituals and practices in order to better understand their culture and therefore allow a therapist to build the type of rapport that is necessary for successful therapy. This research mentions the concept of devil possession and its place within this community at present, and it investigates the importance of understanding the clan and its rituals, especially singing and clapping, as a necessary framework to use during therapy.

The book also mentions, briefly, how the authorities are dealing with the "integration" of Romany culture into mainstream Spanish culture in order to achieve harmony between these two different communities. I support the view that working with Romany people is more effective than trying to impose a different way of life on them, one that will only bring insecurity and anxiety into the Romany community, therefore increasing their isolation from modern Spanish society. Positive discrimination on behalf of institutions is a better method of integrating this community than just Flamenco dancing.

A Brief History of the Romany People

Understanding other cultures is one of the most difficult things that human beings ever have to do. Our prejudices and limited knowledge will always be obstacles that are difficult to ignore and difficult to overcome. My interest in Gypsies is due to my ignorance and curiosity. Regardless of the fact that we share the same country and that they are part of my cultural background, I realised that I did not know them at all. In fact, this research will show that although Gypsies (Romany people) have travelled through our lands for many centuries, we know very little about them.

I will refer to them as the "Romany people" or "Gitanos" because the word "Gypsy" may be understood to mean "traveller, and the reader might interpret these words in a different way, relating to poverty and lack of legal rights. The Romany people in Spain are far from fitting these definitions, and to show respect to them I will address them as they have requested – "Gitanos".

Finally, in order to be consistent with both new research about the origins of this "exotic" culture and the old theories, I have chosen to study three authors to describe Romany culture. I am aware that there is a lot of literature and I may not cover all the studies done on the subject, but I had to settle on two different views in order to present an intercultural approach to the Gitanos' way of healing in a modern society.

Origins of the Romany People

There is no total agreement among historians about the origins of "cultura Gitana" (Romany culture). The popular view is that Romany people came from India, but new research shows that that is not the case. Certainly, they lived in India, but their culture is quite different from Indian culture.

Sandor Avraham (2005) claims that the origins of the Romany people are more Hebrew than Indian. His study uses cultural and religious aspects to explain the origins of the Romany people, rather than taking the linguistic approach which defends the idea of an Indian origin, due to the linguistic similarities between "Romany" (the Romany people's language) and Indian dialects. Avraham writes as follows:

"Concerning language, it is very likely that Roma already spoke an Indic tongue before they reached the subcontinent and that such language was Hurrian, adopted during their first centuries of exile in the land of Mitanni." (Sandor Avraham 2005; 32)

The author also describes how Romany people are

not from India but from Mesopotamia, in the Euphrates Valley. During the Semitic expansion into the Orient Media, an "Accadia" family went to Canaan and then Egypt. In this country, the exiled family grew into thirteen tribes. Twelve of them became the Tribes of Israel, while the final one was dedicated primarily to spiritual activities. Differences between the tribes broke the kingdom in two: northern tribes were culturally closer to Egypt and they used the head of a deer to represent their only god. They also believed in inferior deities. The other tribes formed the Kingdom of Juda in the south of the country.

In 722 B.C., the Assyrians invaded the country and absorbed nearly all the population, except the farmers, into a land called Hanigalbat-Mitanni. There, a language similar to Romany was spoken, while their deities were Indra and Varuna. This land was High Mesopotamia and the natives were Hurrians. In this new land, the proto-Gitanos' identity grew, as Sandor Avraham (2005) describes in his study.

The Romany people kept their rules, their purity rituals, and their belief in only one god. They went to India during the Persian and Macedonian invasions, and they took from these new conquerors the adoration of fire and their belief in magic. It is interesting to point out that, as Sandor Avraham writes:

"The exiled people, formerly Israelites and now simply 'men', Rom, were very gifted in such arts, and understood that practising them was profitable, so these elements were adopted into their own culture, but mainly concerning their behaviour towards the others, the Gadje." (Sandor Avraham 2005; 30)

The reason for leaving that hospitable land and going to India is not very clear, but after that, Romany history is a story of constant exile from one country to another. The reason, as given in other cultures, was: "as a punishment from God for not being hospitable to Virgin Mary when she was in labour giving birth to Jesus".

The Spanish Romany People: Los Gitano

Francisco de Sales Mayo (1870) points out the different names that the Romany people have been given in different countries. In Persia and Turkey they are called "Zingaros", in Russia and the area of Danube, they are named "Zinganes, England knows them as Gypsies, French people refer to them as "Egyptians" and "Bohemians" (from Bohemia), while in Germany they are called "Zigeuner". All those names have something in common: they refer to the River Zind, Sind, or Ind at the west of the Indic peninsula. Spain, in the old days, simply called them Egyptians, but in time, due to phonetic deformation, the word "Gitano" became their popular name. "Zincales" or "Romany" was the word that the culture's population used to address each other.

Los Gitanos came to Europe in the first half of the fifteen century and there is a written record of them from around 1417. At the same time, they were seen around the North Sea, Hungary, and a year later in Switzerland. According to Francisco de Sales Mayo, Los Gitanos went to Europe via two routes: either following the Saracen armies on the African Coast or following the Turkish invasions that led them to Hungary and Bohemia.

Los Gitanos were used to help with transport and with the sacking of the villages during the invasions, but never to fight; their culture is and was peaceful, so much so that they never fought amongst themselves in wars. Sales de Mayo thinks that this is the reason they spread all over Europe – to avoid the confrontation between the different groups of Romany people that followed the Tartar Emperor and the Turkish Sultan Bayaceto I in 1402 (De sales de Mayo 1870).

At the end of the fifteenth century, los Gitanos were considered different from Muslims. El Gitano (the typical Gitano man) has long black hair and is tall and slim, while la Gitana (a Romany woman) has black, shining eyes. They lived in forests, close to rivers, or in the mountains thanks to their mobile homes, "vardos".

Their culture was a skilful, craft-based one. They bred horses and worked metals, such as iron. It is well known that Fernando Segismundo, King of Granada, used their projectiles against the Turks at Funfkirchen.

The women crafted baskets and wooden shoes. Las Gitanas told the future to non-Gitano women, in what was a mystical and very Catholic society. Their ability to please others and their empathy led them to be envied by other cultures.

Some Gitanos received the favours of kings, leading to political envy. In 1499, this, together with the disapproval of the Catholic priests, led to an order of expulsion from the different kingdoms of what is now Spain, following in the footsteps of the

Hebrew culture in 1492. This marked an end to the possibility of the Gitanos running a guild or craft. Gitanos were unable to settle in one place for a long time, or even return to one, because their lives were at risk. Having said that, Sales de Mayo writes:

"…y cualquiera que pudieran ser las animosidades que concitaran, tenían en su favor un escudo maravillosos: su pobreza." (De Sales de Mayo 1870;5)

The author claims that, regardless of the horrible persecution they endured, what kept them alive was their ability to give up everything and move on. Their poverty and their way of life were influenced by their philosophy of "nothing is for nobody and everything is for everybody", and this helped them to survive the hate and envy of other cultures.

Europe followed the example of Spain and started

to throw los Gitanos out of their lands. Los Gitanos were accused of black magic, witchcraft, and even cannibalism.

It was only with Felipe II that things started to change. The Romany people were invited to his wedding to Isabel of France. Los Gitanos danced during the public festivities. Their persecutions were over, and in 1560, Felipe II created rules for the Gitanos, meaning they were able to camp close to villages and towns. It is said that those rules gave birth to "la gitaneria" (gypsy life) or suburban streets inhabited only by Romany people. They were also allowed to go back to their old guild.

Sadly, these peaceful times did not last long; with Felipe III, the Romany people were once again banished from Spain. Years later, under the reign of Felipe IV (in 1633) and Felipe V, Romany people were forbidden from getting married among themselves, to speak their language, or to wear their traditional clothes.

With the arrival of Carlos III in 1783, they recovered their freedom to work and marry among themselves. They were protected at work if they were harassed or not paid. Despite not being permitted to speak their language or wear their traditional clothes, it was the first time that los Gitanos were declared equal, "subdita", to others.

Los Gitanos were considered a different race at that time, which explains why sometimes people still use the expression "la raza Gitana" (Romany race) rather than "la cultura Gitana" (Romany culture). In this book , I will refer to the "cultura Gitana" in order to avoid confusing the reader by mixing the terms culture and race. Besides, those concepts are quite complex and it is difficult to present different writers' viewpoints in a very short written explanation.

La Cultura Gitana (Romany Culture)

When the Romany people spread across the globe, they had a folk culture, according to Francesc Botey. They were also aware of the differences between their origin, language, and customs and those of other cultures. These differences formed a culture in itself, derived from a very small number of people who were very strong in their beliefs and their sympathy for other Romany people's adversity.

Botey calls attention to how quickly Romany people speak when they recognise and talk to each other. They are very sure of their own existence as foreign in the world and yet they are very proud of their differences from other clans of Gitanos.

"Race is a projection towards the future" as Botey explains, it is a simple hereditary combination in a close medium; consolidated by segregation and fixed when inheritable characteristics cross and reproduce inside a group until it creates diverse biotypes quite different for each caste. This explains why different Gitanos tribes and clans are different regardless of their similarities in origin. Suma Fernando (1991) prefers to use the term "ethnicity" and he writes:

"Moreover, races and cultures are no longer linked to geographical locations or types of environment; many societies are both multiracial and multicultural; and concepts of race and culture are being combined and absorbed into that of ethnicity" (Fernando 1991;10)

The theory that it is culture which makes race and not the other way round may not be applicable to the Romany people; culture and race have become one thing.

The Romany man is a "Rom" (meaning "man"), and in a social context, there are seven big groups of "Rom" (clans): Lovara, horse breeders, considered the upper class of the Romany people; Tshurara, dedicated to sacking and war; Matshwaya, merchants, together with Kalderash, dedicated to craft and working with metals (iron). Finally, Sintis, Manush, and Gitanos were outside any castes and they mastered music, dance, and entertainment as an inferior social class (Botey 1977;41).

At the end of the XX century, Spain had mainly Gitanos but also Sinti people in Cataluña and Andalucía. In this book, they will be called Gitanos or Romany people regardless of the true historical and cultural differences among clans, but it is important to recognise their caste system as an explanation for the isolation between clans of Gitanos. They did not organise marriages between some clans, and also they did not gather all clans together for their festivals.

La Familia Gitana (Romany's Family): El Clan

The Gitana family is a patriarchal one; that is to say, the man, Rom, is the head of the family, making all the decisions and organising the economy for the clan, tribe, or family. In Spain, the word "pueblo" (people or group of people) is used to show that it is more than a single family but less than a tribe. Therefore, in this article, the word "clan" will be used to describe the Romany people in a social context.

The family has a very important role for the reciprocity of affection and the place of an individual inside the clan. They are never alone, always in small groups, and their clan is not a geographical concept. Relatives are all over the country, which explains why they are unpredictable in their travelling; going to visit their blood brothers is a necessity. There is only one kind of person in their society – "Rom" (men) – and they are all equal and free, but they all need their link to the clan. The clan is reduced and self-sufficient, very respectful of age and sex. Their solidarity and strong relationship is peculiar to the Spanish Gitanos. There is no "you and I", only the community: the Gitano looks after the others and others look after the Gitano. The clan is ruled by three main laws (De Sales de Mayo 1970):

1. Do not separate from the Gitano (Romany man).
2. Be faithful to your Gitano (husband).
3. Pay all your debts to the Gitano.

The cultura Gitana (Romany culture) is about unity: work, life, religion, and art are seen as a whole; there are no fractions. The Gitano is an artist. He may be understood as lazy, but from the Gitano's point of view, "El Payo" (non-Romany people) work against him. Moral values, not economic values, make somebody "good", and any possible animosity towards them is erased by a strong feeling of belonging to the clan.

There is no different kind of work in the family context. You can see the Gitano cleaning and the woman looking after the horse. Only in maternal issues, such as custody of the virginity of the young girls (lacha) and looking after the elderly and ill, may women be more involved. Very early in life, the young Gitana is taught the importance of not losing her lacha (virginity). In order to fulfil her role as guardian to the young Gitana, the mother will make her wear special underwear called "dicle", which is not removed until the night before the wedding day.

In this patriarchal society, there is a very important role for a woman – "la abuela" (granny) is the wife of the head of the family. She has authority in all domestic affairs.

Francesc Botey explores the great importance of how the Gitano identify with nature. Their link to the natural world, for example, made them very skilful at drawing maps. They never had a form of cosmology and their explanation of the world is deeply related to the Bible, on a smaller scale, because at the end of the day "Rom" and his clan are the most important things in the world. It is prudent to mention that more therapists are acknowledging the importance of family maps to uncover the family's interpersonal dynamics. R. Jozef Perelberg reinforces the idea of family in therapy by writing:

"A family map may contain contradictory ideas and principles at different stages of the lifecycle; these may be held by the different members in the family." (Perelberg 2000; 129)

The Gitana family was and still is a hierarchical one; each person has a role in a network of social relationships. This understanding of the family and the world agrees with the description that Sandor

Avraham gives of the Romany people in general. According to this author, their cultural and spiritual characteristics can be divided into two categories:

1. Beliefs, laws, rules, and traditions very similar to ancient Hebrew traditions

2. Beliefs related to fire and other systemic beliefs of this kind are mainly used as a link to non-Romany people, the "Payo" world.

The word "belief", in this context, is understood as an acceptance of a thing, fact, or statement as being true or existing (Concise Oxford Dictionary 1988). This is not a fixed culture, but it helps them to understand that their individuality exists in the context of family and clan.

Intercultural Aspects of Healing in the Cultura Gitana (Romany People)

The cultura Gitana (Romany people) are well known for healing their own. Until the last three decades, they never used modern medicine. The word "healing" will be used in this article to describe a process that restores the lost balance of body and mind; Rom is a unity in contact with nature and this "exotic" culture is very much connected to it.

Although the Romany way of healing, using knowledge of herbs, is important, it is perhaps more interesting to analyse the community and personal healing based on the Romany people's beliefs about themselves in the world. It is not the intention of this research to ignore the cultura Gitana's valuable knowledge of traditional herb-based medicine, but it is also important to acknowledge the rituals involved in their traditional way of healing within their community. Some of the practices listed below are lost and others are very much still in use at the present time.

Palmistry and Fortune-Telling: Bahi (Buenaventura)

Palmistry is defined in George Borrow's study as the determination of the physical and intellectual abilities of an individual by looking at the lines in his/her hands. Those lines (lifelines) are related to the heart, genitals, brain, kidney, stomach, and head.

The Romany people used this knowledge for fortune-telling, which satisfied the needs of non-Romany population when they required reassurance and comfort at times of great doubt and anxiety.

It may not be their own creation, but the Romany people are considered the best at telling the future.

The Gitana (Romany women) were accused of telling ladies what they wanted to hear in order to gain their favours and increase their own profit, but having said that, the Gitana do offer a great service as healers. Gitana, a very patient woman, had the gift of calming an afflicted heart; many Gitanas were consulted in love and business matters.

It is important to mention that they used their fortune-telling abilities only on non-Romany people, on the grounds that all Gitanos have this ability, as Raymond Buckland explains. Some authors posit that they never used these healing methods because they did not believe in them, suggesting instead that this is how they made themselves useful to the society and was a way of showing their need to manipulate the environment they lived in.

There is no doubt that Romany people have a gift for listening to others and they were (and still are) natural modern psychologists, especially when you consider all the good they have provided by giving attention and hope to their "clients".

El Mal de Ojo (The Evil Eye): Querelar Nasula

"Querelar nasuna" means to make someone ill through a simple bad look. Historical records show that this practice is as old as Hebrew culture. In fact, it is not unique to Hebrew and Gitano cultures; the capacity to harm with your thoughts and looks has appeared in many primitive cultures around the world. In the old days, it was thought you could kill someone with a fatal look. In Andalucía (the southern part of Spain) the amulet of a horn from a deer was the most common protection against the "mal de ojo". The evil eye was more effective while the "victim" was eating or drinking and that is why it is still considered rude to visit someone unannounced at those times. Also, it is more powerful when done by a woman than by a man (Borrow 1932).

Romany Poison: The "Drao"

The "drao" was more than a way of healing, it was the manner through which the Romany people made themselves feared and respected. Romany people were capable of preparing a poison for the cattle of any farmer that did not show kindness to them, striking their livestock ill or even killing them. It was also a trick to present themselves as the only people with the knowledge to cure the cattle, for a very small price. These actions stopped quite quickly and there were few Gitanos capable of preparing the "drao". In order to cure the poisoned cattle, the Gitanos used their famous magic spells. All this gave them status as a people with great knowledge – how to cure nearly any ailment among the Payos (non-Romany population) and therefore they became highly respected, at least until the Payos found out about their tricks.

La Bar Lachi (the Magnet Stone)

George H. Borrow (1932) claims that the magnet stone is the most important belief for the Gitanos. They thought of it as a miracle stone which protected the person from everything, even death. The stone is more powerful in its natural state, but it is harder to find. Also, it was very important for the witches to be able to perform their ritual of love on someone; a wedding is always a path to happiness for the community.

Community Healing: La Boda (the Wedding)

The young Gitana gets married at fourteen years old to a Gitano, who is usually older than her and chosen by her parents. In the twenty-first century, this practice is still very much alive.

George Borrow describes a typical Romany wedding in his book. Under Cale laws (ley Gitana), before the actual wedding, there is a public "esponsales" (betrothal) ceremony in which the couple promise to love to each, and they then have to wait two years for the wedding day. During those two years, the young couple are allowed to talk and to give presents to each other, but they are never allowed to see each other alone in the countryside or outside the village or camp. Any suggestion of a sexual relationship before the wedding will lead to public shame for both families.

It is interesting to note that the Romany community has no fear regarding their daughters being involved with Payos. The young Gitana could go out with her friends and with Payos without limitations due to their lack of sexual interest in these men of "white skin".

The actual wedding day is a very important event not only for the couple but for the whole community. From a therapeutic point of view, this ceremony helps to restore balance in the community and bring peace and happiness to its members. It also brings an economical debt to the father of the groom.

Another important event in this ceremony is the examination of the "dicle" and the "lacha" of the young Romany girl. Four elderly women are chosen (two from her side of the family and two from the side of the groom's family) to inspect the virginity of the young Gitana; if she is still untouched, the wedding will take place the following day, but if her virginity is not clear, the bride has to disappear. There are a lot of rumours about the fate of non-virgin girls; some people think they were killed, were moved into different communities, or that they simply ran away and mixed with the Payo population.

The dicle is shown to the community in order to demonstrate the girl's honesty, and then the "Fiesta" starts. For the next three days, the community will enjoy the best wine and food that they can get. The music is heard all over the place and their Flamenco dance and songs take over from the ordinary conversation of everyday life. The ceremony is open to any Gitano, and strangers are welcome, provided they are Romany people.

With regards to funerals and the concept of death, there is a description of the Romany customs in Raymond Buckland's study (2003). The ill Gitano will die in a designated tent called a "bender"; this tent is also used during the birth of a baby. The community carries on as normal until the death takes place; it is then that grief and crying are shown in public. The dead are put into a wooden box and buried in a forest with their favourite items and their work tools. Grieving and remembering the dead varies according to the group of Romany people. Some Romany groups need a month to celebrate a funeral, others need only three days, but common to all is the importance of music and singing in showing their feelings and respect for the dead.

The Romany Witch and Wizard: Shuvihani and Shuvihano

The Romany witch and wizard are respected for their knowledge of life as much as their magic practices. The word "shuvihani" is more related to a wise and judicious woman (or man) with knowledge. They are capable of aiding or harming, according to their wishes. It is believed that a shuvihani is the union of a young Romany person with the spirit of water or earth. The young shuvihani will learn how to use this gift under the supervision of an elderly shuvihani. There is no ceremony or special clothing needed in order to become a "shuvihani", only the wisdom to believe in the power that nature gives.

There are three kinds of spirits: air, earth, and water. Romany people consider the earth spirits the most friendly and good, while water and air spirits could cause harm. There are also ghosts and vampires called "mullo". A mullo is a Gitano who has died due to a curse cast by another Gitano.

Chamanismo (Shamanism)

Shamanism is a very important part of this culture,

as it is for Siberian, African, and Australian tribes. The chaman (shaman) is different from a shuvihani, but you could find a Gitano practising both roles in a community. They are capable not only of healing body and mind, but also of gaining knowledge from their ancestors and telling the future. The shaman needs to follow a path called a grai (horse). It is the vehicle for his spiritual journey that leads him to knowledge. The symbolism for this relationship between shaman and knowledge is represented by a tree and a wooden wheel.

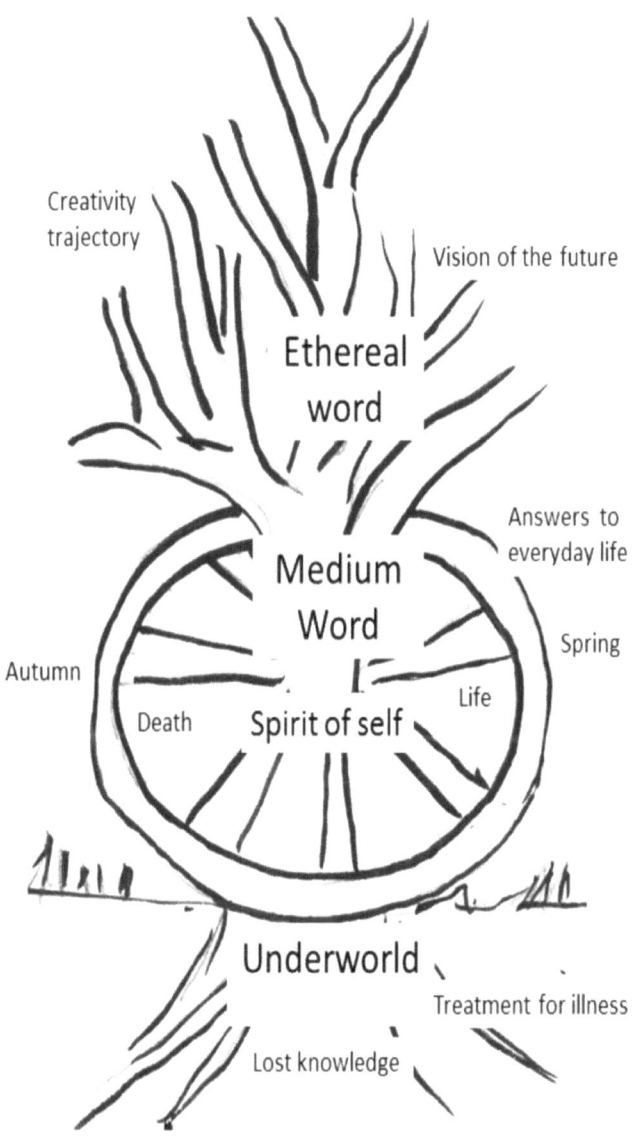

Inspired by Raymond Buckland

Modern Beliefs: la Iglesia de Filadelfia (Evangelical Church).

At the present time, the Gitanos are posing a challenge to those promoting their integration into the Spanish society. Some regions of Spain have ordered the Gitanos into regulated housing and education for their children; failure to comply would mean they would have to move on somewhere else. This is the way in which the authorities have decided to appease the worried non-Gitano population who come into contact with the Romany way of life. By helping the Gitanos with funding, the authorities hope that the claims of robbery and drug dealing might stop, leading to a change in the way the non-Gitano community views Romany culture.

The "Gitano" word for this housing is associated with "chavolismo", which means a collection of buildings badly finished without electricity or water facilities, supervised by the council. They are mainly located at the entrance to big cities, close to the motorways. Such estates are not very pleasant sights because there is often rubbish close by and in some cases there are no public toilets. Also, they give a false impression of very serious poverty issues in the cities. The Gitanos are not a specific victim of poverty in Spain; instead, their lifestyle is more related to the need for a nomadic freedom.

The group of Gitanos I have been in contact with are from the Basque Country, in northern Spain. This group is particularly friendly and very welcoming. They are located in Alza, close to the main city of San Sebastian. Their church is in the ground-floor basement in a block of flats and it is decorated in pastel yellow and pink. Few things hang on the walls; in fact, only the Catholic cross. Aside from the atrium where the pastor speaks, there is a set of classical and very modern electric guitars, as well as some drums and a microphone. The church was formed in 2009 and keeps the formality of women sitting on the right, men on the left, while the children (chavvis) are permitted to sit anywhere until they are fifteen years old, at which point baptism takes place and the young Gitano has a role in the religious community (singing, praying, or speaking).

Mr. Juan Hernandez and Mr. Antonio Dual are the "pastores" of the church. The members go every day except Tuesdays and they celebrate the "pacto del pan y el vino" (communion) on Sundays. It is different from the Catholic tradition because they have to go to church every day in order to remind themselves that they are followers of Jesus Christ at all times. The "pacto" of bread and wine is just as symbolic an act as for non-Gitano Catholics, although they do not believe that it is the body and the blood of Jesus as Catholics do.

In this modern community, the figure of

"patriarca" no longer exists in its traditional form. Now, the patriarca is someone elderly who gives advice to the young and helps to keep the peace among the young Gitanos. In southern Spain, the patriarca has the role of representative to the associations that are in place around the country. This community in particular is mostly made up of relatives, but other churches are bigger (there are six more in the area) and they have Payos attending their services. This church also visits other evangelical churches, such as the Bautista Church, to share their songs and support their faith.

In my opinion, this religious community is of vital importance for the social integration of the Romany people into Spanish society for two reasons. The first is that the non-Gitano population have a chance to see them in a more positive light, ruled by some moral principles and in normal flats, becoming known by and integrated into the community in the area. Secondly, the Gitano feel part of a community united by spiritualism; they need a non-materialistic reason to stay in one place for a long time and the Filadelfia church helps them to channel that need for a sense of belonging in a positive way. The young Gitano use the church as a place to meet with other Gitanos, and they are monitored at all times by the elder. The elder is the most respected man in this community after the pastor, due to his being wise, calm, and experienced.

This community does not follow the traditional beliefs named in the first part of this article, but they do know of them through their mothers. They use the Seguridad Social, a national health service, when their children are ill or experience an injury, although if the illness is thought to be related to the soul (Alma), they would be more likely to confide in their pastor, who then decides what action to take. There is a very particular illness that modern doctors are powerless to treat – the pastor is the only one who can cure it: possession by evil.

Evil is very much alive for this community of Gitanos and Satan is evil's master. Satan is a fallen angel, the enemy of God. The pastor is not only a moral guide and a (Lutheran) Bible reader, but is also a therapist to a community in contact with their good and bad spirits. Women are never pastors but they are a very important part of the rituals.

Inspired by Curnow Vosper

Mr. Antonio Dual, a pastor for twenty-five years, has performed an exorcism. "Satan is very much alive and He is very clever", Mr. Dual claims. Satan has the ability to fool the best of the "pastores" (priests) and sometimes it takes more than three days to make Him leave someone's body.

As Dr. Angela Hobart said in a lecture (2005), therapists have the responsibility to: *contain the pain of the client, empower the client to enable the healing to take place, engender trust,* and, finally, *to empathise with the client's situation.* A pastor has a similar responsibility for his community when an exorcism occurs, but his approach is more intercultural. First of all, Romany people do not believe that all mental illnesses are based in childhood experiences, as many people from other cultures do. They believe that society has a lot to account for as well. Lack of moral guidance in this modern world is very much a cause of these ills from their point of view.

There is no childhood or cultural pressure that can be blamed for possession, as it is a very personal thing. It is not very clear why some individuals are possessed and others not, but Antonio Dual emphasises the need to let the word of God into your heart at all times, and also to understand that anything that it is said or done by him is through the influence of God.

Possessions are as old as human history. They are the process through which a spirit takes the body of a human being and controls it. The spirit that originally inhabited the body will not remember anything of the possession. Exorcism is the healing ritual through which Satan or the demon that possesses that body is removed. It started in the thirteenth century with the approval of the Pope as part of a spiritual act. The first exorcism that any Christian undergoes is during their baptism.

In this book, I will only be describing the therapeutic aspect of the healing process on a possessed person. Antonio Dual makes it very clear that there are differences between possession and mental illness. When a member of the community is suffering from mental illness, they are taken to the hospital, where they receive proper medical care. Mr Dual clarifies that it is clear when a demon or Satan is in possession of someone's body. The possessed person acts very differently from usual. They reject all contact with God, the church, religious music, the pastor, and their friends. Their behaviour can be very aggressive, towards others or towards themselves. They often scream and may fall to the ground, kicking and shouting words that insult God or do not make sense to others. Their faces change and no conventional medication can help because that body simply becomes a mediator between the world and the demonic spirit.

The healing process takes place in the local church with the pastor and three more experienced "pastores" from other churches. There may be some women present but they have to be elderly, with previous experience. Their role is to sing and clap with the music. Singing is very important to this community, not only as a celebratory act but also as a healing act. The pastors will pray and read the Bible and ask the demon spirit to leave the body, holding their right hand up while their left hand is holding their side, next to the heart. The duration of this act depends on the demon and how strong it is, but Mr Dual said that the strongest he had seen withstood three full days of constant prayer, even through the night. After the exorcism ritual, the person is very peaceful. They feel physically tired and will never forget that it could happen again.

As has been said, Gitanos believe in spirits of good and bad forces. Any member of the community can become possessed by the Holy Spirit. This is another form of possession, but in this case it is a positive one. The possessed person will not harm himself/herself but will talk "in tongues" (or glossolalia). In this community, this kind of possession is called "*Inspiración del Espíritu Santo*".

Inspired by Wilfredo Lam

Felicitas D. Goodman (1988) claims this kind of possession can only come about when very specific preconditions are met. The first one is the *Spirit's Fingerprint.* According to the author, spirits will only enter the body during the right ritual; for the Gitanos, praying in the church is the first step. The second is the *Spirit's Key;* the ritual preparations are very important in order to summon the spirit. Hymns and different decorations are part of this process. And finally, the *Spirit's Door* which is a person in "trance or ecstasy". Trance is defined as a state of higher consciousness that a human can achieve. It is interesting to point out that some researchers believe that the ability to go into this particular state of consciousness is genetically transmitted and is in all of us. It is also clear that the trance is consciously induced and therefore is also a learned behaviour. To trigger this state of altered consciousness, a ritual is needed in most cases.

Filadelfia church offers rituals that will enable their members to have an *"Inspiración del Espíritu Santo"*. Although Mr. Dual says that it is the Holy Spirit who comes to you, not you who calls to Him, it is clear that the member has to be "clean" in his/her heart. According to the pastor, this act can take a few seconds or minutes, it depends on the Holy Spirit, but the possession finishes with the member fainting and falling to the ground. A few minutes later, he/she will feel fulfilled and full of happiness; there is a transformation.

Many cultures understand that this kind of behaviour does not indicate pathology at all, and they see very clearly the difference between this possession and a psychotic episode from a mentally ill person (e.g., multiple personality syndrome). When the behaviour is related to a mental illness, it is not under any kind of control and so it happens at random. Possession occurs according to defined rules and under certain circumstances (Goodman 1988; 17).

Arthur Kleinman (1981) determines few categories that practitioner–patient relationships have in common, across various cultures. I understand "practitioner" as the healer (in this case, the pastor), and the ill patient. The first category is the *Setting*, the place where the healing process will take place. The second category involves characteristics of the *Interpersonal Interaction*; that is to say the number of people involved in the healing process, the time and the length of the treatment, the language used among the participants, and their attitude towards each other. The third category is *Idiom of Communication*: types of language used such as naturalistic, spiritual, psychological, singing, etc., and if the patient is using words considered conflicting, tacit, open, or sharing, etc.

The fourth category is *Clinical Reality*, which includes concepts such as sacred or secular, disease-oriented or illness-oriented, symbolic or instrumental interventions. Also, therapeutic expectations and responsibility of the carer should be considered.

Finally, the fifth category is *Therapeutic Stages* and *Mechanisms*; this involves the place where the healing is taking place; it also involves the organization and structure of the healing processes, and the mechanisms required for the change to take place. All this must be evaluated if the patient is to benefit from healing. The author recognises the therapeutic power that a shaman or priest has in containing crisis in a family or community, which could lead to an "illness".

Conclusion

Romany culture has presented a challenge to the Education and Health Department of Spain as they attempt to organise ways to facilitate the integration of Romany culture into Spanish society. The Education Department have to understand that the hierarchical nature of a Romany family makes them very protective towards their children. Some schools allow Romany children to arrive late (e.g., Colegio San José, calle Prim) in order to help them become more involved in a modern society. The fact that Romany parents will not let their children go on excursions with the school is a sign of this protective nature rather than selfishness, and nowadays most teachers are aware of that. Often, teachers do not impose the rules of the school on these students but build up mutual trust; in this way, the Education Department hopes to see more school integration in future generations.

The Health Department is not so understanding and willing to compromise. However, if a member of a clan is in hospital, the number of visitors permitted at one given time is larger than the recommended number by doctors (two visitors per patient).

It could be claimed that the pastor in the Gitanos community is a great healer of the insecurities and anxieties that members of that community may have. Here is someone who cares, understands and resolves a crisis or conflict, either personal or within the clan, and it is not wrong to consider the possibility that psychiatrists and psychologists have to work with the Gitano healers rather than against them.

Suman Fernando said in a lecture (2005), *"You work with your patients from their beliefs and not from yours"*.

Religious beliefs and other ways of healing are in some ways more established than modern science, and for many people a belief in science is also an act of faith. George S. Howard writes as follows:

"So scientific and humanistic thought do represent separate and non-comparable modes of knowing because they have evolved to fit different intellectual, ecological niches. And, just as one would never say, for example, that a squirrel was a better animal than a chipmunk, one should not make the bold assertion that scientific insights are superior to the wisdom of the humanities." (Howard 1991; 189)

At the end of the day, we all have to understand that flamenco is not enough to integrate the cultura Gitana into mainstream Spanish society (or into any other European country), and it is everybody's responsibility to find a way to live together while respecting each other's beliefs.

Map showing the original land where Sanskrit language was born inhabited by Hurrian, Scytho-Sarmatic and Aryan peoples.

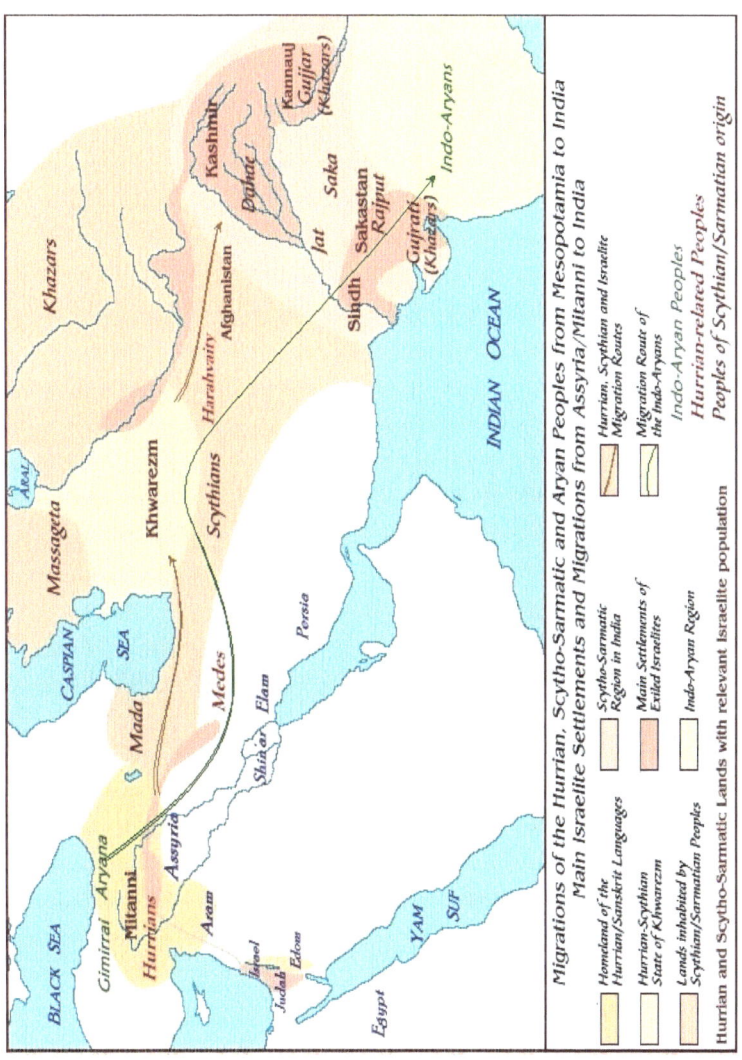

Avraham, Sandor web page: *Myths, hypothesis and facts concerning the Origin of People.*

Notes

Sandor Avraham 2005, www.imninalu.net/roma.htm, p. 40.

Sandor Avraham 2005, www.imninalu.net/roma.htm p. 32.

Sandor Avraham 2005, www.imninalu.net/roma.htm

Sandor Avraham 2005, www.imninalu.net/roma.htm p. 30.

De Sales de Mayo, F., 1870, *El gitanismo: historia, costumbres y dialecto de los gitanos*

De Sales de Mayo, F., 1970, *El gitanismo: historia, costumbres y dialecto de los gitanos. p. 5.*

Fernando, S., 1991, *Mental health, race and culture. p. 10.*

Botey, F., 1977, *Lo gitano: una cultura folk desconocida.* p. 41.

De Sales de Mayo, F., 1970, *El gitanismo: historia, costumbres y dialecto de los gitanos.*

Perelberg, R.J., 2000, 'Familiar and unfamiliar types of family structure'. In *Intercultural Therapy.* p. 129

The Concise Oxford Dictionary, 1988

George Borrow, 1932

Lutheran Bible

F.D. Goodman, 1988, p. 17

Howard,G.S., 1991, 'Culture tales. A narrative approach to thinking, cross-cultural psychology.' *American Psychology.* March, p. 189

Drawings
Designers: Nerea San José and Edith Jones
inspired by
Wifredo Lam
Salem by Sydney Curnow Vosper (1908)
Raymond Buckland

Bibliography

Avraham, Sandor web page: *Myths, hypothesis and facts concerning the Origin of People.* www.imninalu.net/roma.htm

Borrow, George H. (1932): *Los Zincali (los gitanos de Espana).* Madrid, La Nave.

Botey, Francesc (1970): *Lo gitano: una cultura folk desconocida.* Barcelona, Nova Terra.

Buckland, Raymond (2003): *Hechizos y Magia Gitanos.* Barcelona, Obelisco.

De Sales Mayo, Francisco (1870): *El gitanismo: historia, costumbres y dialecto de los gitanos.* Madrid: Librería de Victoriano.

Dein Simon (2004): 'Working with patients with religious beliefs'. *Advances in psychiatric treatment* (2004), vol. 10, 287-295.

Desjarlais, Robert R. (1996): 'Presence' in *The performance of healing.* C Laderman and M Roseman, London, Routledge

Fernando, Suman (2003): *Cultural diversity, mental health and psychiatry: the struggle against racism.* Hove, Brunner-Routledge

Fernando, Suman (1991): *Mental health, race and culture.* Macmillan, Mind Publications

Goodman, Felicitas D. (1988): *How about demons?: possession and exorcism in a modern world.* USA, Indiana University Press

Hobart, Angela (2002): *Healing performance of Bali:*

between darkness and light. Oxford, Bergahm Books.

Howard, George, S. (1991): 'Culture tales. A narrative approach to thinking, cross-cultural psychology', *American Psychologist*, March, 187-197.

Kleinman, Arthur (1980): *Patients and healers in the context of culture: an exploration of the borderland between anthropology, medicine and psychiatry*. California, University of California Press

Littlewood, Roland and Lipsedge Maurice (2004): *Aliens and Alienists*. Hove, Brunner-Routledge

Littlewood, Roland (2000): 'Towards an Intercultural Therapy' in *Intercultural Therapy*. Edit. Jafar Kareem and Roland Littlewood, Blackwell Science

Levi-Strauss (1972) 'The effectiveness of symbols' in *Structural Anthropology*. Penguin Books

Perelberg, Rosine Jozef (2000): 'Familiar and unfamiliar types of family structure' in *Intercultural Therapy*. Edit. Jafar Kareem and Roland Littlewood, Blackwell Science

Turner, Victor (1966): 'Liminality and Communitas' in *The ritual process: structure and antistructure*. Ithaca, Cornell paperbacks.

Other publications
The Little Workbook of Meaningful Listening

If you have enjoyed the book, please leave a review and share your thoughts.

Where to go next? You can take one of my Online courses

Contact details:

www.listen2earn.com

www.ahypnoticsolution.com